An Awesome

Cousinship of

_____ & _____

Written by

_____

Table of Contents

Foreword

God made us cousins because He knew our mothers could not handle us as siblings.

Chapter 1

The First Time We Met

The first time we met was the day

_____

_____

_____

Although I don't remember much, but I knew that

_____

_____

_____

_____

_____

Back then, I was _____ (age) and you were _____ (age)

When we met, I

_____

because

_____

_____

_____

_____

_____

_____

Cousins:
Childhood playmates who grow up to be forever
friends

Chapter 2

You In My Eyes

Five words or phrases that come to my mind when I think of you:

1.

———————————————————————————————

2.

———————————————————————————————

3.

———————————————————————————————

4.

———————————————————————————————

5.

———————————————————————————————

Born as a cousin, made as a friend.

Chapter 3

My Best Memories Of Us

Of the many embarrassing things we have done together, this one stands out in my mind the most:

_____

_____

_____

_____

_____

_____

_____

_____

_____

_____

_____

I remember when I was

_____

_____

_____

_____

_____

_____

_____

_____

_____

_____

_____

_____

One of my favorite fun times with you was

_____

_____

_____

_____

_____

_____

_____

_____

_____

_____

_____

Do you remember when

_____

_____

_____

_____

_____

_____

_____

_____

_____

_____

_____

_____

I will never forget how funny it was when

_____

_____

_____

_____

_____

_____

_____

_____

_____

_____

_____

_____

I will never forget the moment of us when

_____

_____

_____

_____

_____

_____

_____

_____

_____

_____

_____

_____

_____

I still can't believe that you

_____

_____

_____

_____

_____

_____

_____

_____

_____

_____

_____

I remember

_____

_____

_____

_____

_____

_____

_____

_____

_____

_____

_____

_____

On my_____, I remember that

_____

_____

_____

_____

_____

_____

_____

_____

_____

_____

_____

_____

I am sorry that

_____

_____

_____

_____

_____

_____

_____

_____

_____

_____

_____

_____

_____

No matter what
happens...
Some memories
can never be
replaced.

Chapter 4

30 Reasons Why You Are An Awesome Cousin

1. I like your

_____

2. You are my favorite

_____ in the world

3. I like hearing stories about your

_____

4. I like how talented you are at

_____

5. I like to watch you

_____

6. You definitely deserve the

_____award

7. You have the greatest taste in

_____

8. You make me want to be a better

_____

9. I love to

_____with you

10.   I believe the world needs your

unique_____

11.   I am so glad that you like my

_____

12.   It is so funny when you

_____

13.   I like it when you

_____

14.   I never get tired of your

_____

15.   I love how you never get tired of my

_____

16.   I like it when you wear

_____

17.   I am kind of obsessed with your

_____

18.   I like how you

_____everyday

19.   I like how you

_____

20. You know exactly what

_____

21.   I know that

_____

22. You are

_____

23.   I can tell

_____

24.　You give the best

_____

25. You're the only person in the world

who_____

26.   Just by looking at you!

_____

27.   It's the worst when

_____

28.   You understand

_____

29.   You never

_____

30.   Together, we would be

_____

I like you, because you join in on my weirdness.

Chapter 5

I'm Grateful For You

Everyday, I am grateful that you

_____

_____

_____

_____

_____

_____

_____

_____

_____

_____

_____

I'm so thankful for the moments. So glad I got to know you.

Chapter 6
Photo Memories

These are some of my favorite photo memories of us together ☺

_____

_____

_____

Insert Photo Here

Insert Photo Here

_____

_____

_____

_____

_____

_____

Insert Photo Here

_____

_____

_____

I love those random memories that make me smile no matter what is going on in my life right now.

Chapter Infinity

Because of you, I had an amazing childhood that I will never forget.

_____

_____

_____

_____

_____

_____

_____

_____

_____

_____

_____

_____

_____

Don't get one of those lame greeting cards from a store that will likely get lost after awhile. Get your loved ones something more meaningful that will put a smile on their faces every single time!

www.loveydoveygifts.com

Made in the USA
Lexington, KY
24 January 2017